CROSSINGS

Creating Fun:

Recreation, Sports and Hobbies

by Kathy McGovern

For my husband, Ben,
the holiest and most playful person I know

Living the Good News, Inc.
a division of The Morehouse Publishing Group
Editorial Offices
600 Grant Street, Suite 400
Denver, CO 80203

Cover Design and Layout: Val Price

Printed in the United States of America.

The scripture quotations contained herein are from the New Revised Standard Version Bible, copyright © 1989 by the Division of Christian Education of the National Council of Churches of Christ in the USA. Used by permission.

ISBN 1-889108-38-3

CONTENTS

Foreword

Ah, fun. You've waited for it, saved for it, spent *way* too much time fantasizing about it. And now it's here! The surfboard is sanded, the snowboard is oiled, the multi-purpose vehicle is packed and gassed and chained and straining to go. You've got your sunscreen, umbrella, beach cushion, all-weather tent, kayak, bungee cord and bicycle pump. This is it! This is what you've worked eleven months and two weeks for. So...are we having fun yet?

Having fun these days can be pretty exhausting. The demands on people today mandate that they love the outdoors and be in triathalon shape at all times. Those exuberant twenty-somethings doing backflips off the canyon cliffs into the roaring river (and never spilling a drop of their Mountain Dew) can be a very tough act to follow. What exactly is fun for you? Figuring that out is more than half the battle.

Ever feel especially miserable while in the pursuit of recreation and fun? Maybe that's because all that fun isn't re-creating you at all. Fun should make you healthy and happy and at peace. It probably even promotes healing, inside and out. This book will offer some suggestions for helping that happen, and yes, we'll have some fun along the way.

This resource is meant to help you and your friends reflect on the place of fun and recreation in your lives. There truly is a "spirituality of fun"—a deep connectedness with God when we are at play—that we may sense somewhere inside but may never have "put words around." This is your opportunity to share, with yourself and others, who you truly are, for we are never more ourselves, and never closer to God, than when we are totally given over to re-creation. "Joy," said C.S. Lewis, "is the very serious business of heaven."

Throughout the book you will be given a chance to talk with each other and with yourself. Take advantage of the Group Discussion Questions and the Group Activities. You might be surprised at what you'll learn about those serious-looking people in your group. They just might be closet air-guitar players when they think nobody's watching! As you spend time with the Individual Reflection Questions, you may surface some important insights into your own needs and desires for true rest and play.

The Bible has much to say about the human creature (and God) at play. In fact,

> Scripture begins with a garden in the cool of the day and ends with a city at play; so play—art and celebration and fun and games, and a playful spirit—is part of our calling, part of the creation mandate. It is not the play of self-indulgence, nor of shed responsibility, but of gladness, and celebration in responsible relationship to God. Play requires a free spirit, rather than free time, a spirit freed from thinking and acting as if life itself depended altogether on me. The Christian can afford to play.[1]

We can afford to play, but most of us have forgotten how. This means, sadly, that we are forgetting how to be human, for "play is not the key to being human, but being human the key to play."[2]

As we investigate this "spirituality of play" we will look at the ways in which our society tries to work the play instinct right out of us. We'll try to remember the magic moments of our youth when fantasy and festival were the bookends of our days. We'll provide some "theological reflection" on fun, and remember how desperately we need to waste more time. Chapters four through six explore the ways "twenty-some-things" reported they most enjoyed spending their free time. (Few surprises here—being in the outdoors with friends is still the number one way in which these young people say they feel connected with God.) The final chapter will review what we've learned and offer some of the thoughtful insights of some of the young people with whom we spoke.

Many beautiful young people shared with me, through letters and phone calls and personal interviews, their memories of themselves as children and the ways in which they have fun today. I am especially grateful to Mary Frances and Bill Jaster, the directors of Denver's wonderful Colorado Vincentian Volunteers. By putting me in contact with their extraordinary corps of young "Generation X" volunteers, who have come from all over the country to live and work in friendship with the poor, I was invited into an ever-widening circle of happy, restless, responsive young adults who have found creative ways to play while doing some deadly serious work.

I offer, too, my lifelong affection for my favorite "twenty-somethings", my delightful nieces Julie and Sarah. Ever the San Diego "valley girls", ever the absolute essence of sun-burned, windblown beach bums, they will be, for me, forever young. Despite the California trappings of their recent years, they will always be the ecstatic little girls in our home movies, racing the sled up and down their Colorado hillside, laughing and jumping and being, effortlessly, exactly who they were meant to be—the glory of God, the human person fully alive.

In talking to the many young adults who participated in this book I always noticed a certain sadness when the time for our conversations ended. Hours could go by, yet no one seemed to tire of remembering the play of childhood, or laughing with friends over the ways they have found to have fun in this work-clogged world. May you find the same pleasure, the same re-creation, as you share with friends and group-members your own insights into yourself as a playful person. Often, at the end of a session of laughter and poignant con-versation, as we were packing up to leave, one or another of the interviewees would say, wistfully, "Gosh, this was fun."

Notes

1 Arthur F. Holmes, "Towards a Christian Play Ethic,"
  Christian Science Review (1981), vol. 11, no.1, 46-47.

2 *Ibid.,* 44.

CHAPTER ONE
Hey You! You Work Too Much

"Each day, and the living of it, has to be a conscious creation in which discipline and order are relieved with some play and pure foolishness."
—May Sarton, Belgian-American writer

In this chapter we will look at the issues of overwork in our society, and some of the reasons for it. We will look at the evolution of the North American work ethic, and ask ourselves some hard questions about our need to bury ourselves in work. Reflection questions, group activities and a prayer activity will follow at the end of each chapter. As you read, keep in mind this question:

○ Does God love me because I am a beloved child, or because of the work I have completed so far in my life?

The Erosion of Leisure

It seems downright silly now, but twenty years ago, people worried about what we were going to do with our free time. The technology of the late twentieth century was supposed to free us from many burdens of making a living.

Their predictions would have been right, if we had chosen to work fewer hours for the same level of productive output. We could be working only six months of the year...instead, we chose to increase the amount we own and consume by twofold. The major loss has been in our free time.[1]

CREATING FUN

And so the question has *not* been, as many feared, what shall
we do with all this free time, but, instead, what happened
to it?

In her widely noted book *The Overworked American*,
Harvard University economist Juliet Schor reported that since
the late 1960s the average worker has seen his or her work
hours increase by the equivalent of one month a year:

> The erosion of wages is also a factor: 80 percent of
> American workers must put in an extra 145 hours, or at
> least six weeks a year, just to reach their 1973 standards
> of living.[2]

The assumption that we live in the most leisured society in
history is woefully off the mark. Leisure was actually more
plentiful in the medieval era, the so-called Dark Ages, when
time was ruled not by the factory clock, but by the Christian
calendar:

> The extent and prevalence of holy days at that time was
> staggering from the point of view of what we have today.
> In England, which had the hardest working people of
> the European countries, workers had about a third of all
> days devoted to festivals or holy days. In Catholic coun-
> tries, it was greater. Spain is estimated to have had
> five...months devoted to feasts and holy days. All of these
> were feast days which the peasants took by custom. They
> were important local traditions.[3]

The word "holiday" takes its meaning from "holy day," and the church of the Middle Ages, with its cycle of saints and feasts, provided lots of time for celebration and fun. So what happened? Why do we work so much today? While North Americans seem satisfied with their measly two-week annual vacations, European laws allow the French, Germans and British to take a minimum of five to six weeks of vacation every year.[4]

Why Are We Workaholics?

The North American work ethic has its roots in our frontier past. None of us can yet take for granted the back-breaking work of our forebearers, much less the long and often thankless work days of our own parents. Think of the *work* that it has taken to forge this country into the world leader it is today.

> Once here, the colonists faced the awesome task of conquering the wilderness. Woods and forests to be cut. Huts, houses and warehouses to be built. Land to be worked and cultivated, crops seeded and harvested. Then, from east to west, the frontier moved from one cutting edge to another, across rivers, prairies, hills and mountains. The eastern boundaries of the country moved west with roads, inns, canals, wagons and settlements.[5]

So it probably makes sense that somewhere in the primordial past of a 24-year-old woman in Montana lives a hardy great-great grandmother whose spirit somehow compels her to put in those long, hard work hours during the day. The irony is that today's technology allows her to work, unlike her ancestress, all night too.

Today's young person has had to compete on several levels. High school seniors know their college applications have to out-dazzle all the others if they are to be considered for scholarships. Straight A's have never been enough; they must show outstanding community service and be captain of the swim team to make it into the running. Once in the job market, they then have to compete with their parents' generation for those increasingly rare positions that offer benefits and stability. Stuck in what have been dubbed low-level McJobs, many young people find themselves working longer and harder, for less, than the generations before them.

But the Bible is clear about the intended balance between work and re-creative rest, as we shall see throughout this book. For example, the rhythm of work and rest is laid out in the Fourth Commandment: "Six days you shall labor and do all your work; but on the seventh day...you shall not do any work" (Exodus 20:9-10).

Which makes one wonder, if ancient peoples in a subsistent society were willing to let go of the plow every seven days, why aren't we?

Group Activities

○ Make a pact with three other people, in which you each promise to check up on the others for a period of one month. Weekly phone reminders (at the office!) will help keep each other honest. The person who works the least overtime and weekends at the end of the month gets taken to dinner and a movie by the other three.

○ Schedule a fun activity with one other person twice a week at 5 p.m. Walking, in-line skating, ice cream eating...the winner is the one who cancels the least often in the course of four weeks. Excuses like dentist appointments and dinner with Dad don't count—we know you're really sneaking back to the office.

Group Discussion Questions

○ What kind of work schedules do we keep? Why? Do longer hours equate with more productivity, or make people more valuable employees, more indispensable human beings?

○ What pressures in our workplace are causing us to overwork? Can those pressures be addressed? If not, why not?

○ Are we taking our cues for overwork from our parents? Are we happy with the way our parents' careers affected our lives?

Individual Reflection Questions

Rate yourself on the following scale. One means you
"strongly agree;" five means you "strongly disagree."

1	2	3	4	5

1. My self-esteem is directly proportional to my work output.

2. Even though people tell me not to overwork, they're secretly hoping I'll fail at my job.

3. My parents made my life happier because of their overwork.

4. I actually am more at home working than being at home.

5. I am willing to give up recreation for monetary remuneration.

6. My friends will think I am a "slacker" if I don't overwork.

7. There are so many needs in this world; who am I to think I'm entitled to a weekly day of rest?

8. Jesus worked every day of his life.

9. I secretly disdain people who don't work as hard as I do.

10. I've forgotten how to have fun.

Individual Prayer

Go to a quiet, secluded place during your lunch hour (at the office, at school, at home). Find a way to do this reflection alone. (If you are a student, adapt these questions for your own situation.) Review your workday so far by prayerfully considering these questions:

❍ Have I been a good, productive employee so far today?

❍ Do I know my job well enough to get things done on time?

❍ Are my skills compatible with this job, or will I forever be running behind?

❍ Am I energized today, or stressed by the workload and my inability to catch up?

❍ Did I observe a sabbath rest this week?

❍ How can God help me better balance my human need for rest and recreation?

Pray: First of all, provident God, thank you for the work you have given me. Thank you that I have the health and the means to make my way in the world. I thank you for the many blessings of this workday. Thank you for the friendships, the shared missions, the shared energies. I pray for every person at my workplace, especially those most in need of your grace today. O God, I ask for your wisdom in my

15

work. Give me the skills to do it well, and the grace
to walk away at the end of the day. Give me the
peace of knowing that I have done my best in the
time allotted me. If that time is not enough, I pray
for the gifts to do my job more efficiently. If that is
still not enough, then I ask for the strength to keep
this work in proper perspective, knowing that you
created me to be a whole person, a joyful person.
Please help me keep my life in balance, O God.
Amen.

Further Resources

Helen Doohan, "Burnout: A Critical Issue," *Journal of
Religion and Health* (Winter 1982), vol. 21, 352-358.

Gordon J. Dahl, "Time, Work and Leisure Today," *Christian
Century* (February 10, 1971), vol. 88, 185-189.

William McNamara, O.C.D., "A Cure for Noise," *America*
(December 7, 1996), vol. 175, no. 18, 22-23.

Gregory J. Millman, "Monks Say Work American Style is
Hazardous to Monastic Life," *National Catholic Reporter*
(September 6, 1996), 3-4.

Notes

1. Edward Vacek, "Never on Sundays; Whatever Happened to Leisure?" *Commonweal* (February 11, 1994), vol. 121, no. 3, 13.

2. Juliet Schor, *The Overworked American: The Unexpected Decline of Leisure* U.S.A.: HarperCollins Publishers, 1991), quoted by William Bole, "Work Without End, Amen," *Our Sunday Visitor* September 1, 1996), 6.

3. *Ibid.*

4. *Ibid.,* 82.

5. Victor F. Hoffmann, "Work, Leisure and the Center of Life," *Lutheran Quarterly* (August 1970), vol. 22, 232-233.

CHAPTER TWO
The Spirituality of Play

"Very little is needed to make a happy life. It is all within yourself, in your way of thinking."
—Marcus Aurelius, Roman emperor and philosopher

"We are not human beings having a spiritual experience. We are spiritual beings having a human experience."
—Teilhard de Chardin

This chapter will offer several different reflections on the way our play shapes us spiritually, and our spiritual life shapes our play. Through the writings of saints Theresa of Avila and Don Bosco we will see the ways in which leisure and play form us and bring us closer to God. As you read, ask yourself:

○ Am I a playful person?

○ How can I regain the holiness of play?

What Is the "Spirituality of Play"?
We all know what play is. It's stepping into that place where we can laugh, enjoy easy companionship, and move away from the rigors of responsibility for a time. Play happens when we decide to look at things with a humorous eye. It's what a baby does when adults leave the room. It's what adults do when a baby crawls into it.

Gwen Wright offers this explanation of spirituality:

Spirituality, then, is not limited merely to those in a specific category, nor to those of a particular religion or culture. It is available to all of us, even though it may take different forms according to our religious beliefs.[1]

Our word "spirit" is a translation of the Hebrew words *ruach* (wind), and *neshamah* (breath), which are used in the Old Testament:

Without breath, like a gentle wind moving through our bodies, we die. The Spirit is the breath of life; it is that quality of life which gives vitality. Spirituality likewise gives life vitality, and a spirituality that has as its basis the belief that humans are created good, and in the image of God, is a vital spirituality.[2]

To be *vital*, then, is to be full of the Spirit. Think of the young man David, striking the harp and making music for God, or of Jesus comparing the kingdom of heaven to a great wedding feast (Matthew 22: 1-14). These were *vital* people, *holy* people, and, as we shall see in the final chapter, even playful people.

And, as it turns out, *healthy* people are people who can play:

When we keep inside us fear, anger and sadness, we also keep inside us happiness and joy. For example, the same muscles that control the explosion of deep laughter control those of sobbing. The belly muscles can produce "belly laughs" and crying that shakes the whole body. Similarly, anger is often experienced as pain in the lower back and constriction of the belly and lower back muscles. Joy and ecstasy are experienced as a letting go of rigidity throughout the body.[3]

Playful people are healthy people, made in the image of God, that playful creator of the world. But play requires a certain state of leisure, and here we turn to Joseph Pieper, probably the foremost twentieth-century writer on the subject:

> Leisure is not the attitude of mind of those who actively intervene, but of those who are open to everything; not of those who grab and grab hold, but of those who leave the reins loose and who are free and easy themselves— almost like a person falling asleep, for one can only fall asleep by letting go.[4]

Letting Go

To "let go" is to be at leisure, which allows us to play, which makes us holy. That sounds simple enough, except that:

> Most of us don't even know how to relax, much less how to enter into a way of life that relates leisure to a deepening intimacy with God, one another, and ourselves. Leisure is one of the main streams in the flow of spiritual life.[5]

This kind of "leisure" enables us to get a few friends together for a game of softball, or a night of country line or swing dancing. It's the leisure of meeting a friend for lunch, or a cappuccino while dozing off in the cozy corner chair at the bookstore. It's the leisure of summer walks in the evening with the neighborhood kids, topped off with an ice cream cone. It's coaching the co-ed T-ball team. It's dropping in on friends for no reason at all. It's taking the bike instead of the car, just for fun.

Theresa of Avila's book *Interior Castle*, described by Leonard Doohan, provides a model for spiritual growth that includes leisure as an essential ingredient.

> As one progresses through the seven mansions of the castle, the fourth mansion provides a place for the prayer of quiet. Here...we find the place for leisured recollection in which mind and imagination are not distracted by busyness. This practice of leisured recollection is critical to the process of conversion, a process...impossible without an open attitude to God and a willingness to take time to encounter our own neediness. Leisure, often associated with wasted time and shameful idleness, is actually the ground necessary for our growth as saints.[6]

So, play, recreation and even prayer come from a person "properly leisured."

It also brings to mind the charisma of Don Bosco, one of the great Salesian saints of the nineteenth century. Don Bosco is beloved in the memory of the Church because of his warm and loving relationship with young children. Because he himself had had a difficult childhood, he dedicated himself to the education of youth, who loved him and responded to his playful spirit. When asked about the secret of his success, he talked about that "letting go":

I don't know what my system is. I go ahead and make use of circumstances and inspiration from the good God.[7]

Some of his sayings about his approach to education are delightful to recall:

Try to keep the balance between freedom and pure discipline. Get rid of boredom; join pleasure to duty. Don't worry about a small outburst of enthusiasm; join in the noise. If the noise is, by chance, necessary for the merry-making, whip it up. Joy is indispensable, in the school and in the church.[8]

A spiritual person is a joyful person, a person who, as the next chapter will show, has wasted lots of precious time with children and friends and cloud formations. How do you measure up?

Group Activities

○ People have always believed that God sends good things and blessings in our sleep. The Book of Job says "God giveth songs in the night" (25:10). Keep track, for two weeks, of your dreams. Keep a notebook by your bed so that you can keep track of those fleeting dream memories. Then share some of the recurring themes in your dreams with your group. Do you sense anxiety in your dreams, or exhilaration, or a sense of peace? Does this tell you anything about your sense of leisure in your waking hours?

○ In a related exercise, keep track of your sleep habits. Do you get enough sleep? When do you get the best, most restful sleep? Are you a light sleeper? Heavy sleeper? Do worries keep you awake? Share your findings with your group, and share advice about how to get the best sleep.

Group Discussion Questions

○ When was the last time you remember "playing"? It could be enjoying a great joke or climbing a great mountain.

○ What is *your* definition of play? What do *you* love to do? ("Brady Bunch" reruns count. This is *your* play, no one else's!)

Individual Reflection Questions

○ Play should always be re-creative. We should feel refreshed and renewed after a session of "play." What is re-creative recreation for you? When do you feel the most renewed?

○ Do you feel a connection with God when you are at play? Can you imagine God there with you in your happiest moments of "letting go"?

Group Prayer

As a group, take a silent walk around a two-block area. Every person can go at his or her own pace. In thirty minutes, return in silence. Some will have walked the two blocks several times; some will never have gotten past the first set of houses. In a prayerful atmosphere (perhaps a circle in which everyone is sitting) each person offers a reflection of thanks for something that had gone unnoticed before. This becomes a prayer of thankfulness for the leisure that brings contemplation!

Further Resources

Paul Heintzman and Glen Van Andel, "Leisure and
Spirituality," *Parks and Recreation* (March 1995), vol.
30, no. 3, 22-29.

David Miller, *Gods and Games: Toward a Theology of Play*
(New York: Harper and Row, 1973).

Robert E. Neale, *In Praise of Play* (New York: Harper and
Row, 1969).

Josef Pieper, *Happiness and Contemplation* (New York:
Pantheon Books, 1958).

———, *In Tune with the World: A Theory of Festivity* (New
York: Harcourt, Brace & Jovanovich, 1965).

Charles S. Prebish, *Religion and Sport: The Meeting of
Sacred and Profane* (Westport, CT: Greenwood Press,
1993).

Leland Ryken, "Teach Us to Play, Lord," *Christianity Today*
(May 27, 1991), vol. 35, 20-22.

Notes

1. Gwen L. Wright, "Spirituality and Creative Leisure," *Pastoral Psychology* (Spring 1984), vol. 32, 193.

2. *Ibid.*, 193.

3. *Ibid.*, 196.

4. Joseph Pieper, "Leisure as a Spiritual Attitude," adapted from *Leisure, the Basis of Culture,* tr. by A. Dru, 1952, in *Weavings* (March-April 1983), vol. 8, 6.

5. Leonard Doohan, *Leisure, A Spiritual Need* (Notre Dame, IN: Ave Maria Press, 1990), 42.

6. *Ibid.*, 43.

7. Quoted by Leonardo Von Matt and Henri Bosco, *Don Bosco* (New York: Universe Books, 1965), 29.

8. *Ibid.*, 30.

CHAPTER THREE
We Used to be Good at Play

"The events of childhood do not pass, but repeat themselves like seasons of the year."   —Eleanor Farjeon

"We grow neither better nor worse as we get old, but more like ourselves."   —May Lamberton Becker

"In the midst of winter, I finally learned there was in me an invincible summer."   —Albert Camus

"If only we'd stop trying to be happy, we could have a pretty good time."   —Edith Wharton

"Teacher, I have kept all these since my youth." (Mark 10:20)

This chapter will look at children, especially their wonderful inclination to waste time. It will also present several profiles, in which young people reminisce about their childhoods. The farm kids and the city kids have different stories, but they share the same universal common denominators. Fun means friends and family and sun and snow and water and lots of precious time to waste. As you read, keep in mind these questions:

❍ Is the child in me waiting to come out?

❍ Am I mature enough in my spiritual life to waste precious time?

Wasting Time in Childhood

In Jesus' day, children were a population at risk. Like their mothers, they had no protection under the law. How out-of-step Jesus must have seemed when:

> *"People were bringing little children to him in order that he might touch them; and the disciples spoke sternly to them. But when Jesus saw this, he was indignant and said to them, 'Let the little children come to me, do not stop them; for it is to such as these that the kingdom of God belongs.' "* (Mark. 10:13-14)

Children, those notorious underachievers and time squanderers, inhabit the kingdom of heaven, and we're supposed to model ourselves after *them!* Children bring home no paycheck...they bring home injured birds and hungry kittens. You probably know how to shower, blow-dry your hair, grab a granola bar and be out the door in ten minutes. A child hasn't even figured out the snap on his pajama bottoms in that tiny time.

Children cannot be rushed. They need time to investigate the strange shapes the light makes on the carpet, the fascinating pools that spilled milk makes on the table. And *these* are the creatures for whom the kingdom of heaven is reserved! Children know how to waste precious time, and our task, as "grown-ups," is to do the same.

This charism of "time-wasting" is available to the person who is, by grace or conscious choice, open to it. The person who bears a sense of childlike fun and delight is, most probably, a deeply spiritual person, a person who recognizes the importance of wasting precious time. Boston College theologian Steven Pope sees the question of labor and leisure as pivotal to the future of faith and family:

> A lot of people are having trouble in their marriages because they don't realize that having a family requires "wasting" a lot of time—just being together, going to the beach, reading together, taking long walks. That sort of activity rebels against the modern mentality of always looking to get ahead, looking for the next raise, the next promotion. We have a responsibility to create leisure time, to be present with God and neighbor. By virtue of our baptism, we're all called to be holy people, and you can't be holy without leisure.[1]

Profiles

Twenty-two-year-old Sarah K., now busy with a full-time job and a full-time boyfriend, says:

> My childhood was the only time in my life when I actually got to spend time with my sister. Since she was three years older than I was, she was always hanging out with her own friends once she got into junior high. But our childhood was spent with each other, and we had *so* much fun. I had a huge imagination when I was a child. We put on plays, we played "store," we made sandcastles, we laughed all the time. Now that we're grown up we have to make appointments to see each other. But

when we were kids I got to play with her every day. Of all the gifts of childhood, that's the one I miss the most.

So, childhood was rich not only in the *time* we had, but the *time we had to spend with the people who mean the most to us*. As "grown-ups" we can't go to our siblings, or cousins, or childhood friends, and say "Let's play store." But these beloved partners in our childhood, these children walking around in what *we* know are only adult costumes, are always with us, always inside us in memory. The time we wasted with these childhood companions lives on in us, and underpins the awe we still feel at a caterpillar in the rain, or a blue, blue sky with a big fat white cloud in the center. We remember, somewhere hidden inside of us, whole days given over to just such wonders. And, for most of us, we spent those days in the company of our sisters and brothers, our cousins, our neighborhood friends. Such are the simple gifts of childhood, and yet they could be found again if we were willing to waste the time.

Listen to these 20-something Midwesterners, Carla and Mike, recall the time of their childhood. Carla grew up on a farm, one of thirteen brothers and sisters:

> Living on the farm, all of our play revolved around our experience there. We played on hay racks, we played on sandpiles with the tractors. We spent *hours* in the fields making flower necklaces. When I was in the house I used to imagine that the living room carpet was my own field, and I'd separate my territory from my sisters' with

carefully placed shoestrings and socks. That was a whole
day's activity, right there...

Twenty-five-year-old Angela tells this story about wasting
time:

> One of my favorite people, Father David Geib, O.P., can
> be credited with teaching me a sense of fun in cards. As a
> 50-something campus minister, he knows he can reach
> our generation through fun, so playing cards and teach-
> ing people cards is definitely part of his ministry. He has
> a great sense of the spirituality of fun, and he has shared
> that with me. By the way, when I was first getting in-
> volved with the Newman Center I was asked to play cards
> one evening because the group was short a player. The
> card game was in Father David's office. This guy Jim was
> my partner, and we won! Jim and I were married June 1,
> 1996.

The marriage might never have happened if Angela hadn't
consciously "wasted" time with friends that night...

At 25, Carmen is a strikingly beautiful young woman who
has lived in two very different worlds. Born in Honduras,
Carmen's childhood was rich with imaginary games. She
remembers...

> I had few toys until I came to this country when I was
> eight years old. As a result I think I experienced the best
> of both worlds. My brother and my cousins and I played

for hours and hours every day. Our toys were the dirt and the grass, and oh what stories we weaved! I remember the day my cousin went to the neighbors who were pouring cement. He returned with little cement blocks with which he built the most *beautiful* imaginary neighborhood all around our yard. One day I decided the poor ants in our yard must be tired because they had no place to sit down, so I made furniture for them out of the sticks and the grass. Of course that was the easy part...the hard part was getting them to sit down and relax! I also remember the doll houses I made for all my make-believe children. I realize now there is a lot of magic, a lot of deep spirituality in children who are allowed to live in a child's world.

Twenty-two-year-old Lorrette's memories of her childhood in Brooklyn are quite different, but still can bring a warm smile of gratitude:

We practically lived at the park when we were kids. Every day after school, unless it was freezing out, my sister and my friends and I were there. We played softball and kickball, or we just made up our own games as we went along. In the summer we sometimes just sat in the grass. We had a lot of games for inside, too. We'd play "supermarket" and stash groceries all around to put in our carts. We liked to play "office" and pretend we were grown-ups at our jobs. We played *Cagney and Lacey* and pretended we were catching all the bad guys. Which is kind of funny, because for as much time as we spent at the park and in our imaginary lives, I remember being terrified as a child that I would be kidnapped. Such is childhood in the city, I guess. A combination of fantasy and real fears...

Twenty-year-old Greg grew up, as he says, "in the middle of nowhere" in Fort Dodge, Iowa. With farming communities all around them, Greg and his brother had miles and miles of open land to explore:

My mom says I was *constantly* on the move. I walked at nine months and never gave her one moment's peace after that. I started by climbing out of my crib, fell out of the combine at age three, then graduated to climbing literally thousands of trees and rooftops. I remember the challenge I kept giving myself to go higher and higher.

Twenty-seven-year-old Jamal also recalls his lifelong passion for heights:

The thing I remember most is that I was *always* trying to defy gravity. I was always finding things to jump off. When I got a little older my friends and I got into Bicycle Motor Cross(BMX), where you line up a bunch of kids in the neighborhood and try to jump your bike over them. I distinctly remember being absolutely sure that, if I just prayed hard enough, I could fly. I gave myself a good running start and then started flapping my arms...

The funny thing is, I guess I'm still not convinced I
can't fly. Today as an adult I love to jump from cliffs
into rivers, ski-jump, bungee-jump and sky-dive.
Throughout my life I've had dreams about flying. When
I think about the last several years of my life, I wonder if
it all isn't about a deeper spiritual quest...

That magical time of childhood, if we are allowed to live it,
can create, as Cardinal J. Francis Stafford has said, "a precious jewel of memory" that lives deeply inside us throughout
our lives and, with grace, can bring us to God:

In C.S. Lewis's autobiographical reflections *Surprised by
Joy* (1955), he describes several play experiences of his
childhood that pointed him beyond the ordinary hori-
zons of the world. As he gazed at a toy garden landscape
in a biscuit tin, when he smelled a flowering currant
bush...his imagination was baptized. Moreover, having
been surprised once by joy through his play, he was open
for other, more definitive experiences of joy—which cul-
minated in his personal encounter with Jesus Christ.[2]

In her book *Experiencing God With Your Children*, Kathy
Coffey writes:

After a week that had been notably horrible...I sat be-
neath an apple tree in blossom. Its pure beauty was healing, as people find the warm relaxation of sun on the
skin, the many moods in music, the rhythm of waves, or
the fragrance of lilacs. These languages require no vo-

cabulary lists, audio tapes or pronunciation guides. The smallest child can understand their blessings of peace.

Children are also our best guides because their senses, fresh and alive, tingle alertly to stimuli. Their touch has not been petrified; their sight has not yet dimmed; their hearing has not been jaded by overstimulation. They are ripe for a conversation with creation.[3]

And so we hear these voices, these witnesses to the deep power of the childhood we each carry within. Jesus reminds us that we must become "like a little child" (Matthew 18:2), and the child who is truly us whispers "here I am." When we remember and become that child again we are very close to the heavenly Jerusalem, where "the city shall be full of boys and girls playing in the streets" (Zechariah 8:5).

Group Activities

❍ Share with each other your favorite childhood fantasy (being able to fly, being a ballet dancer or a cowboy). How are you still living out those fantasies?

❍ Make a group list of all the precious time you've wasted this week while about the business of re-creation ("Brady Bunch" reruns don't count). See if you can double that list by this time next month.

Group Discussion Questions

❍ What is your favorite memory of the play of your childhood?

○ Are there crossovers from your childhood play to what you enjoy doing today?

○ Did friends or family members play a big part in your fun as a child? Is that still true today?

Individual Reflection Questions

○ How did your parents encourage you to be imaginative and creative as a child?

○ Do you sense that part of you could still regain that sense of wonder, and of play, that you had as a child?

○ If you someday become a parent, how will you help your child retain a child's wonder?

○ What good things can come from wasting time?

Group Prayer Activity

Each person brings to the prayer a memento from childhood (a doll, a ball, a baseball card...). Be prepared to offer a one-sentence prayer of thanks for the childhood that the object recalls for you. For example, one might say "I hold in my hands this soccer ball, kicked and trampled and handled a million times by my friends and me during our childhood. I thank You, God, for this dear friend." After each person has given a personal thanks, someone reads Ecclesiastes 3:1-11a, ending with "God has put the past and future in our minds." The leader then closes the prayer by praying:

"O God of past and future, of yesterday and tomorrow, we hold our memories of childhood close to our hearts. You were there with us, delighting us with the wonders of your world. You are here with us now, again opening our eyes to your presence throughout our lives. May the child of our hearts never lose sight of you. *Amen.*"

Further Resources

Carolyn Hoyt, "Giving Your Child a Spiritual Life," *Parents Magazine* (February 1995), vol. 70, no.2, 95-98.

Maria W. Piers, ed., *Play and Development* (New York: W.W. Norton and Co., 1972).

Marybeth Shea, "The Green Spirituality of Playgrounds," *Sojourners* (December-January, 1994-1995), vol. 23, 39.

Notes

1. William Bole, "Work Without End, Amen," *Our Sunday Visitor* (September 1, 1996), 6-7.

2. Robert K. Johnston, "How Then Shall We Play?" *Christianity Today* (December 17, 1982), vol. 26, 54.

3. Kathy Coffey, *Experiencing God with Your Children* (New York: The Crossroad Publishing Co., 1997), 23.

CHAPTER FOUR
Nature

"Consider the lilies of the field, how they grow; they neither toil nor spin, yet I tell you, even Solomon in all his glory was not clothed like one of these." (Matthew 6:28, 29)

"The heavens are telling the glory of God; and the firmament proclaims his handiwork... their voice goes out through all the earth, and their words to the ends of the world." (Psalms 19:1, 4)

"The earth is the Lord's and all that is in it." (Psalms 24:1)

In this chapter, young people talk about the best fun they have...being outside, enjoying the world. Pope John Paul II agrees, in similar words, about the human need to be out in nature. As you read, think about this question:

○ In the gospels, Jesus is often depicted in the desert, on the lake, on mountains and hillsides. What does his connection with nature tell you?

"Go Outside and Play"
By far the biggest thing that "Generation X" does for fun is to get outdoors and play. This is not a sedentary generation by any stretch. Over and over, young people reported that nature is the place where they most love to be:

> When I was in high school I ran cross-country, and now as a college student I find myself spending more and

more time working things out in my life through long
bike rides and wilderness hikes by myself.   —*Pedro*

As a teenager I was totally involved in outdoor activities.
I ran cross-country and track, I played softball and did
figure skating.   —*Kim*

Since my early childhood was spent on a half acre of
land on a huge lake, being outdoors was my world. We
were often outside as a family—hiking, camping, fishing, building. Those are still the things I love to do today
for recreation.   —*Cherisse*

Growing up on the farm, I was able to run and play
alone or with siblings for hours at a time without my
parents having to worry about my whereabouts. We
would play hide-and-go-seek in the cornfield, build forts
in the hayloft, swing on the tire swing, try to "tame" the
calves to let us ride on their backs, go swimming in the
pond. Even "helping" Dad in the fields or collecting eggs
with Grandma was fun because I loved being outdoors.
                                            —*Tara*

I believe we all need at least occasional exposure to the
beauty, strength and infinite variety of nature to remind
us that our powers truly are minimal in comparison. I've
seen raging waterfalls; trees that seem to impossibly eke
out an existence from the crack in the rock; intricate
patterns in snow crystals, and sand dunes that have been

swept by transforming winds... and a sunset, comet
sighting, full moon and lunar eclipse all in one night!
—*Sarah*

Last summer when my husband and I visited Yellowstone
I found myself laughing out loud at God! This park is
hilarious! From geysers going off all over the place to
bubbling mud pots, it is truly God's playground.
—*Angela*

Two Nature Lovers

Most of the young people we've featured in this chapter would
probably not realize it, but someone rather famous shares
their passion for the outdoors. In fact, in his 1985 "Apostolic
Letter to the Youth of the World," Pope John Paul II begged
his audience not to miss all the grace that nature mediates:

> ...contact with the visible world, with nature, is of im-
> mense importance. In one's youth this relationship to
> the visible world is enriching in a way that differs from
> knowledge of the world "obtained from books." It en-
> riches us in a direct way. One could say that by being in
> contact with nature we absorb into our human existence
> *the very mystery of creation* which reveals itself to us
> through the untold wealth and variety of visible beings,
> and which at the same time is beckoning us towards
> what is hidden and invisible.

It is good for people to read this wonderful book—the "book of nature"—which lies open for each one of us. What the youthful mind and heart read in this book seems to be in perfect harmony with the exhortation to wisdom: "Acquire wisdom, acquire insight...Do not forsake her and she will keep you; love her and she will guard you" (Proverbs 4:5-7).

And so my hope for you young people is that your "growth in stature and in wisdom" will come about through this contact with nature. Make time for this! Do not miss it! Accept too the fatigue and effort that this contact sometimes involves... Such fatigue is creative, and also constitutes the element of *healthy relaxation* which is as necessary as study and work.[1]

Study, work, prayer, play and relaxation are all part of a "holy" life.

At 25, Julie is the fastest female runner of the half-marathon in San Diego. The daughter of a marathon runner, Julie began running her last year in high school. She has run nine miles a day, every morning, for the last eight years. She lives in an apartment two blocks from Ocean Beach. Let's listen to her story:

No words can describe the way I feel when I am out on the beach, running. I still get goose bumps when I remember that scene in *Forrest Gump* (my favorite movie) when he is out running in the desert. All of a sudden the whole screen turns red as the sun sets. The beauty just takes your breath away.

These days I am a weekend warrior. Five days a week I am a complete stress case because of the pressure of my job. But every morning, and especially on the weekends, when I wake up with the sun and admire God's beautiful sunrises, green trees and magnificent ocean I just have to say "Thank You, God. I love this place!" This is when I feel the most connected to God and the most focused in my life.

Even with all the time I spend outside every morning, I have a weekly ritual of going to the beach by myself once a week. That's when I read, or just think. It's a huge, huge part of who I am.

Group Activities

○ This one's easy. Get out there! Take a group field trip to a lake. Go fishing. Spend a night out under the stars and observe thirty minutes of silence together. Climb a mountain. Ride your bikes to a nearby nature reserve. Take your cue from the little creatures and the flying birds you'll see there...just break down and play a little.

○ Much of what we've been talking about in this chapter assumes that everybody is able to do the strenuous physical exercise that being outside often demands. But those who are unable to walk or ride bikes are often the best resources for fun things to do outside. Invite some physically challenged friends to go with you to the park. Experience the beauty of nature from their unique vantage point.

Group Discussion Questions

○ Do you feel peer pressure to be really athletic, and great at all outdoor sports? Does that ever take the fun out of the experience of being outside?

○ Share with the group the most fun you've had this month while out in nature. What made it so re-creative?

Individual Reflection Questions

○ Can I truly enjoy a simple pleasure, like swinging on a porch swing on a summer night while listening to the crickets? If not, do I know why?

○ Complete these sentences:

A. Nature seems to speak to me. I feel close to God there be- cause _____

_____

B. I wish I could spend more time outside, but to do that I'd have to give up _____

_____

C. Like Julie, I too have a beautiful place where I go once a week by myself. It is _____

_____

Group Prayer

This group scripture reading allows you to experience one of the Bible's most lyric passages about the sublime wonder of nature. As a group, gather outside in a circle and, using *New American Bibles*, read together the Canticle of the Three Young Men from the third chapter of Daniel, verses 52-90. Alternate the leader part back and forth from women to men. For example, the women might begin, "Blessed are you..." and the men would answer, "Praise and exalt..." Then the men lead the next blessing, and the women respond "Praise and exalt...."

Further Resources

Barbara Kantrowitz, "In Search of the Sacred: Growth of Spirituality in America," *Newsweek* (November 28, 1994), vol. 124, no. 22, 52-55.

Thomas More, *Care of the Soul* (New York: Harper Perennial, 1994).

Anne and Charles Simpkinson and Rose Solerri, eds., *Nourishing the Soul: Discovering the Sacred in Everyday Life* (New York: Harper San Francisco, 1995).

Note

1. John Paul II, "Apostolic Letter of Pope John Paul II To the Youth of the World," (Boston: Daughters of St. Paul, 1985), 51-52.

CHAPTER FIVE
Sports and Music

"I have fought the good fight, I have finished the race, I have kept the faith." (2 Timothy 4:6)

"C'est l'amour qui chante...love alone knows how to sing."
—Joseph Pieper

In this chapter we'll hear from young people from all over the U.S. about two of the most frequently mentioned ingredients of play: sports and music. We will read the responses of these "tweenagers" (youth in that stage caught between settled adulthood and uncertain adolescence) as they write about the passion they feel for both. As you read, keep track of your own "play pulse" by asking yourself these questions:

❍ What sounds like fun to *you*?

❍ Have you had good or bad experiences with these things?

❍ How much of your own identity is caught up with sports and music?

Sports History
Today's "20-something" crowd has grown up with a *lot* of sports and a lot of music, and they can barely speak about "play" without mentioning them. Sports, hobbies (music tops the list here) and recreation of all kinds are a way of life for the young people who were interviewed for this book.

They come by this fascination honestly...games, dances, music and ceremonials have been with us since prehistoric times.

Early recorded history indicates that the Chinese, Egyptians, Aztecs, Babylonians, and other peoples enjoyed cultural and physical activities. Later cultures, particularly the Greek, held games and cultural art in high esteem.[1]

This Greek love for sports, by the way, is the reason why the author of 2 Timothy (traditionally assumed to be Paul) used athletic imagery in the section on "running the race" that was quoted at the beginning of this chapter. How better to connect with his audience? And Paul goes out of his way to make this point when addressing his audience in Corinth, that ancient Greek port city:

> *"Do you not know that in a race the runners all compete, but only one receives the prize? Run in such a way that you may win it."* (1 Corinthians 9:24)

As we saw in Chapter One, during the Middle Ages the many holy days (holidays) afforded opportunities for games and rest, and minstrels and traveling singers offered entertainment.

The Renaissance revived interest in sports, and Sixteenth century philosophers and educators advocated recreation for its social and educational value.

The New England colonists, in their effort to find relaxation during the long and severe winters, conducted a variety of individual and team sports...[2]

Profiles of Sports Enthusiasts

Whether in the thirteen colonies or the fifty states, participating in sports and following favorite teams is still a big part of being young. At 26, Sandy appears to be at the peak of her youth. An athletic, dark-haired beauty, Sandy is married and the mother of a 14-month-old boy:

> Next to being with my husband, Jim, and our baby, I enjoy playing sports. I love competition and working together for a common goal. Exerting myself physically brings me much happiness as I use my coordination and athletic skills. I also like encouraging and helping others when playing team sports, especially if they don't know how to play, or aren't very athletic.

A 20-year-old expressed a similar thought:

> I love playing football and basketball, but a lot of times the fun disappears because of all the swearing and the nasty way people treat each other during competition. The team I play with now goes out of our way to congratulate the guys on the other side when they've done something especially well. We even pray before the game. That helps me relax into a state of true play.
>
> —*Quentin*

Ann, James and Mike are three of five children in an active family. At ages 27, 25 and 18, their lives are going in different directions. Ann and James are young, career-oriented people in a young town (Denver), and Mike is just starting college. But what remains the same about them is their passion for sports. Their mom talks about her adult children:

> Our kids will play any sport, any time, anywhere. Camping, rafting, skiing, bike rides up to Waterton Canyon...this is their life. To this day their favorite thing is still to just take the football outside and toss it around. Now that Ann and James are out of college they have to work a little harder at making connections with friends. We can't believe this, since it's so out of sync with *our* generation, but James and his friends play *rugby*! And his friends and office pals play on a Rollerblade hockey team. Ann has gone back to coaching softball at her old high school. It's a way of connecting with people, doing something helpful, and, of course, playing sports...

Mountain biking, canoeing, fishing, soccer, volleyball, softball...the interviewees from this generation do it all. They also are big fans of major league teams. Following favorite teams will always be a big part of youth, and many of our respondents talked about getting out to all the games (hockey, baseball, basketball, football) they could. But at least one young woman finds the passion for spectator sports a serious problem in her relationship with her boyfriend:

If I could change anything about Brian it would be his obsession with sports. He needs to watch every minute of every game. I feel lonely and bored. I've tried to fit into his life in this way; I've sat through way more games than I've wanted to, but it's never enough.

—*Sarah*

Music

In fact, if this pool of interviewees is representative of its age group, sports is not the most important hobby of Generation X. It is, far and away, music. Every single person we talked to either plays an instrument, sings, goes dancing and "clubbing," or follows a local band:

Music has a huge place in my life. I play guitar and sing, and I play tuba and trombone. I like U2, Tom Petty, the Beatles, James Taylor and Jars of Clay. I sing in the choir and play in the band at my college. We have this one Bach piece that we do for concerts—-the band stops playing and begins singing in four-part harmony. The audience goes wild and it is just the biggest thrill in the world.

—*Greg*

I am a musician—I started drumming when I was in high school and had loads of fun playing in bands. By the time I was 16 I was playing in nightclubs and absolutely loved it. Today I am also a guitarist, singer/songwriter, and I do one-man shows in coffeehouses. My wife is a singer and plays the piano. Music has always been a big part of who I am.

—*Elton*

All three of my roommates and I love to sing and play guitars. I like folk and folk rock, especially Bob Dylan and Jim Croce. Sometimes when I'm outside by myself I just like to sing at the top of my lungs.   *—Chad*

Music is still my greatest stress reliever. I grew up playing piano and brass instruments, and I still really enjoy listening to and playing music.   *—Tara*

One of the things we all love to do is to go down to the county fairgrounds on Thursday nights and do Boot Scooting (country line dancing). We've got a bunch of fancy spins we've added, and basically we just show off. It's really fun.   *—Mike*

For me, having fun has always involved music. I played French horn for several years, and violin for ten.
                                        —Roxanne

When I have free time I do what makes me happy...like dancing! I love to go clubbing, feel the music inside and just move. It touches my spirituality in a mysterious way. Right now I'm really involved in interpretive dance—- African and Latin-American.   *—Carmen*

Swing dancing has caught on with many of this generation, but alternative music and jazz are big too. Coffee houses are packed with young people who are there for music and friends.

Music is mentioned throughout the Bible as a key element of human existence. We even have an entire book of 150 psalms (songs). But perhaps there is no more poignant remark about music than in Matthew 11, when Jesus laments the hard-heartedness of his generation:

> *"It is like children sitting in the marketplaces and call-ing to one another, 'We played the flute for you and you did not dance; we wailed, and you did not mourn.' "*(17)

Jesus seems to be saying that the human creature, if open to the work of God, is meant to respond to music.

In his book *Only the Lover Sings*, Joseph Pieper reflects on the grace that lives in music:

> The intent here is to make one thing clear: that music, the fine arts, poetry—anything that festively raises up human existence and thereby constitutes its true riches—all derive their life from a hidden root, and this root is a contemplation which is turned toward God and the world so as to affirm them.[3]

So when you thought you were making music, you may have been praying all the time.

Group Activities

○ If your group doesn't do this already, start using more music in your get-togethers. Those songs you sing in church are beautiful in other settings, too. Gather every-one around and lift up your hearts!

○ Don't wait for Christmas to go caroling. Some fall or spring evening, take your flashlights and your music and visit the child-care centers, the nursing homes, the shelters. Music heals at every time of year.

Group Discussion Questions

○ What is your favorite sport to play? Why? Are there happy memories associated with that sport? Are you instinctively good at it?

○ What sports do you enjoy that require solitude? Walking, long-distance running, swimming alone? Do you find that re-creative?

Individual Reflection Questions

○ Do you feel uncomfortable in conversations about sports and/or music, because you feel you have to compete to be the best? Where does that feeling come from?

○ List your five favorite songs. Why did you choose these five?

1.

2.

3.

4.

5.

Group Prayer

This is similar to the prayer in chapter three, where we brought mementos of our childhood. This time, in prayerful silence, gather with a symbol of a sports or music memento that represents that gift in your life. Perhaps you'll bring your favorite CD, or your lacrosse sticks, or your tuba. Going around in a circle each person offers a prayer of thanks, ie: "Thank you, gracious God, for the lifetime of beauty that music has given me. I thank you that I can sing (or dance, or play...). May I always find you near me in my music." After all have prayed, the leader may close:

> O generous God, we are surrounded by all good gifts of your tender love. When we run, or play sports, or play music, may we always know it is you alone who have gifted us so. We wait in joyful hope for the day when spinal cord injuries and paralysis of all kinds will be healed, so that we may all sing and dance together in your kingdom. *Amen*.

Further Resources

Roger Kahn, *Memories of Summer* (New York: Hyperion Publishers, 1997).

Dave King and Michael Kaminek, *The Mountain Bike Experience* (New York: Henry Holt & Co., 1996).

Bill Mason, *Path of the Paddle: An Illustrated Guide to the Art of Canoeing* (Minacqua, Wis.: North Word Press, 1995).

Harry Middleton, *The Earth is Enough: Growing Up in a World of Fly-Fishing, Trout and Old Men* (Boulder, Colo.: Pruett Publishing Co., 1989).

Cal Ripken, *The Only Way I Know* (New York: Penguin Books U.S.A., 1997).

Notes

1. W.C. Eberhardt, "Recreation in the U.S.," *The New Catholic Encyclopedia* (New York: McGraw-Hill Book Company, 1967), 130.

2. *Ibid.*

3. Joseph Pieper, *Only the Lover Sings: Art and Contemplation* (San Francisco: Ignatius Press, 1990), Preface.

CHAPTER SIX
More of Our Favorite Things

"To live is so startling it leaves little time for anything else."   —Emily Dickinson

"It is not how much we have, but how much we enjoy, that makes happiness."   —Charles Spurgeon

"A friend loves at all times..." (Proverbs 17:17)

In this chapter, we listen to many vibrant young people talk about what they love to do. You will also read about the primary importance of meaningful friendships. As you read, ask yourself these questions:

○ What is really fun for me?

○ Do I spend more time doing the things I like to do *less*, and less time doing the things I like to do *more*?

In the previous chapter we talked about sports and music, and their importance in the lives of young people. But many other activities and hobbies enrich our lives, too.

> Gardening, painting, sculpting, drawing, photography, cooking, computers...I enjoy all these creative pleasures in a very amateur sense.   —*Sarah*

> I like to attend concerts, plays, visit museums and travel.
> —*David*

The media has, of course, played a pivotal part in the lives of young people today. Raised on video games and television, most admit that the greatest deficit in their lives is that they haven't read very much. (One particularly honest young man, now an administrator, even admitted that, by age 20, he had read exactly three books!) For many, book reading is associated with school and homework. The further they were from their school years, the more amenable many of our respondents were to reading for pleasure. Annette shares an interesting insight about reading:

> I do like to read and am trying to do more and more of it. I think one of the reasons we Generation X-ers are as unstable, confused and indifferent as we are is because we have no common footing with the generations of the past. Every generation before us admired and learned from the generations preceding it. One of the main ways they learned about life before their own was through classic books...

> But we spend our time figuring out solutions to problems that were solved centuries ago. Reading is our continuity with the past. Now I'm trying to fill in the literature void in my education. I'm reading today what I should have read a decade ago. Older literature like Dante's *Divine Comedy*, and more modern literature by Chesterton, for example, are great ways to understand what a culture is supposed to be.

This is what Sarah reads for pleasure:

> I love to read about the places and things I have grown
> to love, including Chicago, Great Britain, the European
> countryside, jazz musicians such as Louis Armstrong
> and Ella Fitzgerald, health and nutrition, animal social
> behaviors and mysteries, and prayer and spirituality.

Avid readers like David and Angela can count off their favorite
authors and books without a blink of the eye: Scott Peck,
Thomas More, John Gray, Neale David Walshe, James
Redfield, Henri Nouwen, Anthony de Mello, Tom Clancy, Ken
Follett. Spy novels, political thrillers, historical fiction and
books about prayer fill their bookshelves.

But, for the most part, the young people we talked to still feel
ambivalent about reading. They *want* to like it, but, apart
from the newest John Grisham novel, they never seem to get
around to it. They seem to feel the same ambivalence, in re-
verse, about television.

Television, it turns out, was a big temptation for many of this
generation in its childhood. Unlike parents, who were probably allowed to watch way too much TV, many young people
were often put on a restricted TV diet of one hour a day.
Therefore, watching TV became the forbidden fruit. They were
supposed to be outside, "enjoying the beautiful summer day"
as their mothers would tell them, but they were sneaking inside to watch reruns and to play video games. As a result, they

seem to really want to *not* like TV, but lots of them really do. Here are a few of their responses (we'll leave their names off so they can stay in the TV. closet):

> We tape two episodes of *Star Trek* every day and watch them.

> I enjoy TV.: *Seinfeld, Coach, Cheers, Mad About You, Saturday Night Live.*

> Every week my friend and I get together to watch *Party of Five,* and then we cry our eyes out.

> I don't like staying home much, unless it's to watch *Seinfeld.*

> I don't watch TV shows on a regular basis—-most sit-coms are utterly insulting—-but I do occasionally enjoy an episode of *America's Funniest Home Videos.*

One 24-year-old woman spoke for many of the respondents:

> I can find enough to occupy my time so that I have no need for TV that glorifies violence, materialism, power and manipulation of others, especially those of the opposite sex. To surround myself with these images would be defeatist.

Finally, this generation has had a positive experience with theatre. From *Les Miserables* to *Rent,* they've seen it and loved it. Two of the respondents, in fact, Greg and Mike, have been performing in theater productions since high school and hope to continue throughout their lives. It is part of what has formed their strong friendship.

Which brings us to probably the most important ingredient of fun for any person, young or old: friends. Friendship is a key biblical theme, so much so that Jesus, while saying goodbye to his disciples in Chapter 15 of John's Gospel, does something extraordinary for a teacher. He calls his students his friends:

> *"You are my friends if you do what I command you. I do not call you servants any longer...I have called you friends, because I have made known to you everything that I have heard from my Father."* (John 15:14, 15)

The book of Sirach (Ecclesiasticus) has a beautiful poem about friendship:

> *"Faithful friends are a sturdy shelter; whoever finds one has found a treasure.*
>
> *Faithful friends are beyond price; no amount can balance their worth.*
>
> *Faithful friends are life-saving medicine; and those who fear the Lord will find them."* (Sirach 6:14-16)

Listen to young people talk about their friends:

I would never want to be without my friends. With my friends I like to "hang out," go to movies or rent them, go out to eat. When you have a group of friends, each person's energy builds up the whole group.   —*Philip*

Throughout my life my fun times have always centered around my friends. As teenagers we would go to movies, hang out at each other's homes, do wild, crazy things that I realize now were very life-threatening! Today my friends make up the vast majority of my fun times. We often go to coffee shops or happy hour somewhere, or just each other's apartments for meals and good discussions.   —*Tara*

Friends have always been the center of my social life. When I'm with my big gang of friends we all just feel like family. We laugh a *lot*, and about things you'd probably never think were funny unless your friends were there to make the experience so much richer and more fun. Lately we've been doing this great thing. We go camping on the weekends. We camp by a stream, then we all kick off our shoes, put our lawn chairs in the middle of the stream and sit up all night, talking and laughing.   —*Marta*

Her sister Julie adds:

Every weekend we follow our favorite local reggae band, *Common Sense,* wherever they play. In the summer our neighborhood has a huge block party, where they cordon off thirteen blocks for this big street festival. Music, food, sun, walkin' around in your shorts and tank top, and all your friends around you...ah, life is good.

Group Activities

○ Tape *Friends*. Get some pizza. Watch the show and make a list of all the things you can find that are *totally* unrealistic (starting with the size-one figures of all the women).

○ Tape a *Seinfeld* rerun. Get some Chinese food. Make the same list of unrealistic aspects of that show (starting, for example, with the apparently unimportant observation that few of the characters have a job).

Group Discussion Questions

○ What activities in your life are the most re-creative? Is *this group* re-creative for you? Why or why not?

○ What other things do you like to do that may not have been mentioned so far in this book?

○ Just for fun, go around the group and tell one favorite story about something you used to do with your "best friend" from childhood.

Individual Reflection Questions

○ After all this talk about fun and recreation, have I figured out what it is I really like to do? Is it okay to admit that?

○ Who are my best friends? Of all my friends, who do I most hope is still in my life twenty years from now?

○ Have I been a "good and faithful friend" in my relationships? How can I improve?

Individual Prayer

In the privacy of your home, take out that box of old pictures of your friends. Spread them all out, all around you. At one point in your life these friends were important enough for you to have received and kept their pictures (and they probably have one of you in their box somewhere too). As you look at them now, pray a prayer of gratitude for each friend, for what they meant to you in the past, and for their happiness and closeness to God today.

Further Resources

Jon Meacham, "The Truth About Twenty-Somethings,"
Washington Monthly (January-February, 1995), vol. 27,
no. 1-2, 21-26.

Karen Schoemer, "Talking 'bout our generation. (Generation
X has no spokesperson.)" *Newsweek* (December 26, 1994),
vol. 124, no. 26, 32-33.

Afterword

As this book comes to a close, ask yourself:

○ Am I willing to make the changes necessary to keep a sense of play in my life?

○ Is the recreation in my life truly re-creative?

Re-creation

This might be the place to talk about that odd spelling we've been using for "re-creation," Did you ever think about the recreation you have in your life as re-creating you? When do you feel as if your "play" has created you all over again? Here are two responses:

> When I'm outside doing something and I feel the warm sun on the back of my neck...yes, that's when I feel re-created.
> —*Mike*

> I often feel a calmness, a sense of peace when I am having fun with my friends, or even when I'm just out by myself. It's a sense of being connected somehow, in touch with what my unique talents are and how they might fit into the scheme of things. I see recreation as the reward for all the labor of the week, and I feel re-created as I sense that I am a part of the great picture.
> —*Greg*

As we have seen, the Bible is full of stories about key figures at joyful play and rest. In the Book of Proverbs, the wisdom of God is delightfully personified as a young child present at the dawn of creation:

> *"Then I was beside him, like a master worker; and I was daily his delight, rejoicing before him always, rejoicing in his inhabited world and delighting in the human race."* (Proverbs 8:30-31)

In the second chapter of Luke, when we read that Jesus, the young child, "grew and became strong, filled with wisdom, and the favor of God was upon him" (40) we know what "wisdom" means! Jesus was open to the fullness of life.

In the first creation story of Genesis 1, God, like a playful child, "pushed back the earth, made channels for water, lit up the sky, and cried out with delight as each new phase of creation was completed. Once the sea was in place, "God created the great sea monsters and every living creature that moves, of every kind, with which the waters swarm" (Genesis 1:21).

Creation, it seems, was not God's *work*, but perfect play.

Note a few of the passages about rest: At the beginning of earthly history, after performing the work of creation, God "rested, and was refreshed" (Exodus 31:17). When the Israelites came into the promised land they observed the counsel of Leviticus to let the land go fallow every seven years (a sabbath for the land), and to even observe a year of jubilee every 50 years (Levitcus 25). On the first and seventh days of the Feast of Unleavened Bread, as well as on the day of first fruits, they remembered the commandment to "do no regular work" (Numbers 28:18, 25-26).

Even though the Hebrew people were never sure that their crops would be plentiful enough for the year, they were careful to observe their annual religious festivals and sacred days. They seemed to have a sacred sense of rest. Why don't we?

From David dancing before the Lord (2 Samuel 6:14), Psalm 150 urging us to praise God with harp, song, trumpet, tambourines, cymbals and dance (3,4), and Jesus himself performing his first miracle at a wedding party (John. 2:1), the message is clear: we are meant to have life, and have it to the full (John. 10:10b).

Fullness of Life
What is that "fullness"? Different people view it in various ways:

> The media seems to think my generation needs to be entertained, but that's not true. We love to just be with each other, and be alive. —*Carla*

> Advertisers are always trying to sell us "things," but the truth is we are human beings, and so we are made to love simple things. —*Carmen*

> This is what I love: profound conversations about God and life, singing sacred songs, listening, being quiet. —*Maria*

Yes, that for me is the "fullness of life"...to be with good
friends, talking about God's love in our lives.

—*Quentin*

Every day I offer all my joy to God, who gives it back a
hundredfold.   —*Chad*

Twenty-year-old Philip is a sensitive, introspective young
man. We'll close this book with his reflection:

While doing something I enjoy I very often pause and reflect, just momentarily, on what God has done for me in
my life, and, directly, what God has done to make "this
moment" possible for me to experience. When doing
something that renews the body, mind and spirit you are
making yourself fresh and new. If you, as I do, can reflect while participating in some sort of recreation, you
can take in so many wonderful things that have been
created for a special purpose in this world.

Group Activities

○ If you've never tried it, experience the joy of sharing God's
presence in your life with close friends. Don't be ashamed
to say, as some have, that you don't yet have a sense of
God in your life. (God isn't finished with any of us yet.)

○ Try to imagine, as a group, all the billions of varieties of
life that God created. Doesn't it sound like God had great
fun?

Group Discussion Questions

○ What is your favorite way to have fun with friends?

○ What is your favorite biblical passage about play?

Individual Reflection Questions

○ Have I been challenged in this study of play?

○ Do I play enough?

○ Why am I afraid to play?

Individual Prayer

After you have answered the questions in this book, find a quiet place. Light a candle and place the book on your lap. Prayerfully, leaf through all the pages, and ask God to bless all the ways in which you experience play and recreation. You might pray this closing prayer:

> Thank you, God, for revealing yourself to me through play. Help me always to be able to find you when I am alone or with friends, at rest, or at work, or at play. Please continue your work in me, that I may have life, and have it to the fullest. *Amen.*

Further Resources

John S. Mogabgab, "And God Rested: Spiritual Dimensions of
Rest," *Weavings* (March-April, 1993), vol. 8, 6-12.

Notes

1. John S. Mogabgab, "Hilarity: Cheerfulness and Humor in
   Christian Spiritual Life," *Weavings* (November-December,
   1994), vol. 9, 10.

CREATING FUN

My Reflections...